THE

ELISHA PRINCIPLE

by

Mark J. Chironna

Destiny Image Publishers
P.O. Box 351
Shippensburg, PA 17257
"We Publish the Prophets"

ISBN 1-56043-006-0

For Worldwide Distribution
Printed in the U.S.A.

First Printing by Destiny Image: 1990
Second Printing by Destiny Image: 1994
Third Printing by Destiny Image: 1995

Destiny Image books are available through these fine distributors outside the United States:

Christian Growth, Inc.
Jalan Kilang-Timor, Singapore 0315

Vine Christian Centre
Mid Glamorgan, Wales, United Kingdom

Rhema Ministries Trading
Randburg, South Africa

Vision Resources
Ponsonby, Auckland, New Zealand

Salvation Book Centre
Petaling, Jaya, Malaysia

WA Buchanan Company
Geebung, Queensland, Australia

Successful Christian Living
Capetown, Rep. of South Africa

Word Alive
Niverville, Manitoba, Canada

Inside the U.S., call toll free to order:
1-800-722-6774

Preface

There are great days ahead for the Lord's army! My understanding of God and the Scriptures won't allow a "doom and gloom" picture of the future Church. I see revival, restoration and victory; not weakness, anemia and apostasy. Many have been declaring "restoration," "revival" and "a new wave of the Spirit" in describing the Body of Christ, present and future. Some of us have been so "rapture-oriented" that we have resigned the world to antichrist forces. But God is building a Church "without spot or wrinkle" and maturing her in preparation for a glorious consummation with her heavenly Bridegroom, the Lord Jesus Christ!

It has always been the desire of the Lord to have a living organism through which to manifest His glory. Unfortunately, we have frequently presented Him with a languishing organization. Each visitation from Heaven has been intended to establish God's people further and deeper into the revealed truth of His Word. Inevitably, we interpose our natural desires between ourselves and God's spiritual desires, undermining His building process. In Exodus 25:8-9 the Lord speaks to Moses in this fashion: "And let them construct a sanctuary for Me, that I may dwell among them. According to all that I am going to show you, as the pattern of the tabernacle and the pattern of its furniture, just so you shall construct it."

Under the direction of Moses, all things were done according to the command of the Lord; as a result we discover that "the cloud covered the tent of meeting, and the glory of the Lord filled the tabernacle" (Ex. 40:34). The principle revealed here is worthy of our consideration. Visitation (the cloud of glory) did not come until all things were done according to Divine pattern. The key to restoration in the Body of Christ is Divine pattern. In Acts 3:19-21, Peter declares:

> *Repent therefore and return, that your sins may be wiped away, in order that TIMES of refreshing may come from the presence of the Lord; and that He may send Jesus, the Christ appointed for you, whom heaven must receive until the PERIOD OF RESTORATION of all things about which God spoke by the mouth of His holy prophets from ancient time.*

If we relegate these verses to the time after the Second Coming, we ignore the weight of the passage. Peter speaks of *periods*, or *times*, of restoration. If we have chosen to have a nearsighted view of the prophets and assume that they imply restoration in the millennium or for a future Jewish race, we miss the importance of this passage to the Church. The prophets spoke primarily of spiritual restoration. They foresaw an age during which God's people would exemplify the character of God Himself before the nations. Many passages in the Old Covenant describing the glory of God over Zion find their ultimate fulfillment in the Church. "We HAVE COME unto Zion" (Heb. 12:2).

Times of restoration and refreshing have come from the presence of the Lord since the day of Pentecost. Every outpouring of the Spirit since that time has fulfilled Peter's sermon and the words of the prophets. The charismatic renewal has not been an exception. It seems, however, that the current renewal has ebbed and God is planning a new thing in the earth. There is expectancy in the air. The ripened grain is waiting to be harvested. The Lord always sends early rains and latter rains to water the fields of wheat. Clouds are gathering and a rain of glory anticipates bursting forth.

Are we ready? If God is moving, are we moving with Him? Will this next visitation produce lasting effects on the Church and the world? Or will we fulfill the old proverb: "He who forgets the past is doomed to repeat it"? While the charismatic movement was wonderful and exciting and real, many things went wrong. In the midst of it, the crystal clear water which flowed from the Throne was muddied by the hands of fleshly indulgence.

A greater wave seems to be heading for the shore. It

behooves us as the people of God to be prepared and available. This book is written as a word of preparation and admonition. We must learn from our mistakes and press on to maturity in the New Covenant (Heb. 6:1). It is my prayer that the Lord will take the words of this book and breathe upon them by His Spirit. I have endeavored to share the insight He has given me in a clear and concise manner. May He multiply it, as He did the loaves and fishes, and feed the multitudes.

Mark J. Chironna

Introduction

Recounting the journey of Elijah and Elisha from Gilgal to Bethel and then on to Jericho, Jordan and finally Elijah's ascension and Elisha's assumption of his prophetic mantle, author Mark Chironna presents a prophetic challenge to the Church. A spiritually renewed Church must match its life and ministry to *The Elisha Principle* of moving on with God.

Don't look in this little book for a carefully-developed system of theological principles; you won't find it. What you will find is a series of penetrating observations about the reluctance of the Church to move in the present purposes of God. These are coupled with strong admonitions and exhortations for Christians to cast aside complacency and dead tradition in favor of the deeper commitment needed to face the spiritual challenges which lie ahead.

Mark Chironna is a minister motivated by a Divine impatience to see the Church fulfill its destiny. This book should help to infuse all who read it with that same godly impatience.

Don Basham

Contents

Chapter One

The Elisha Principle

At present, the Church is in a transitional period. I would like to compare the recent charismatic renewal to the ministry of the prophet Elijah, and the current transitional period to that of the prophet Elisha. It is my conviction that what is now occurring will, in its fulness, far surpass all that has gone before.

Why have I chosen to title this book *The Elisha Principle*? I see a principle that functioned in the life of Elisha, thrusting him into God's front lines. If we desire to see a great move of God in this decade, the principle which governed Elisha's life must govern ours as well.

What exactly is the "Elisha Principle"? Three times in the opening verses of Second Kings chapter two Elisha declares: "As the Lord lives, and as you yourself live, I will not leave you!" (v. 2,4,6) These words reveal the intent and determination of the budding prophet. Unveiled in this statement is the character of a man molded by the hand of the living God. The hand of the invisible God had so fashioned the inner man that God's workmanship was outwardly evident.

Life in the Spirit is never stagnant. Stagnancy is an indication of death and decay. Stagnant water is unfit to give life. We must continually work out what God is working in us. Elisha expressed to Elijah the idea that as long as God was working within Elijah, he would cling to and embrace all that he had to offer. Eventual separation, however, was inevitable. Elisha said, "As the Lord lives, AND AS YOU YOURSELF LIVE, I will not leave you." This implies that if Elijah was no longer God's instrument, Elisha would move on with the Lord alone. Clinging to a form or tradition when its usefulness is past accomplishes nothing for the purposes of God. We must recognize this and be committed to those things blessed and anointed of Heaven. Once the cloud lifts from above the tent of meeting, we need to move on with it. When the cry, "Let God arise!" was shouted by Moses in the wilderness (Num. 10:35), it was time to pack up and follow the Shekinah glory. Practical daily situations are no different. The greatest hindrance to the moving of the Spirit is not the devil, but the Church!

Some of God's people were totally untouched by the charismatic movement. The "good old days" were far better. We could spend all our lives pining for the "good old days" and never embrace fresh visitations from God. Many could not accept sovereign visitation in the form of long hair and faded jeans. The thought of any denomination other than the Pente-costals having the Pentecostal experience was "unscriptural." In *A Midsummer Night's Dream*, the elfin Puck declares very aptly, "Lord, what fools these mortals be!" May God help us to be adaptable and pliable in this hour. May He give us the spirit and determination of Elisha to say, "As the Lord lives, and as you yourself live, I will not leave you."

In Second Kings chapter two, Elijah the fiery prophet re-ceived notice from the Head Office to depart. Retirement bene-fits included a free ride to Headquarters on *Out Of This World Airlines.* His arrival was not unlike his departure. When Elijah first appeared, he simply came out of nowhere (1 Kings 17). Without any credentials, ordination papers, or a license to preach, Elijah boldly declared that God would not send rain until he told Him to do so. (The land was then in a time of drought.) Who does this pompous, arrogant, self-made preach-er think he is, anyway? A prophet? This was the reaction of the undiscerning ear, but to those who "had an ear to hear," the Lord was rendering recompense to a rebellious nation.

The charismatic movement seemed to come out of nowhere. In the early 1900's the fire of Pentecost began to blaze from prayer rooms in Kansas and California. The Azusa Street Re-vival became the rallying point for the contemporary Pente-costal outpouring. Spirit-filled believers began to declare that God was visiting His people with a "latter rain" of glory, preceding the coming of the Lord. The Book of Acts came alive!

This visitation was not without resistance and persecution. I enjoy listening to stories of some of the old-timers at our church. Some of them were threatened even to the point of death! Many were asked to leave their own churches because, in the eyes of unbelieving leadership, they had embraced a heretical doctrine. This occurred in America, Canada, areas of Europe, Norway and Sweden, Australia and New Zealand. The Assemblies of God were birthed during this outpouring. Great men and women of God today were considered heretics and troublemakers to evangelical fundamentalists of that day. Men such as Charles Price, Smith Wigglesworth, John Lake, the Bosworths, Mary Woodworth Etter and Aimee Semple MacPherson (to name just a few) ministered with great power and authority.

In the late 1940's God visited a small group of farmers in North Battleford, Saskatchewan with a glorious outpouring of the Spirit which became known as the "latter rain." Spontaneous praise, worship and prophecy were earmarks of the revival. What started with a few people up in a frozen, isolated region spread like wildfire. God revealed many principles of revival that touched the hearts of thousands.

God again visited the earth with power and glory in the late 1960's. Thousands of young men and women, disgusted with the "establishment," found refuge in drugs, sex, rock music and communal living. Astoundingly, with no apparent prompting, they began to call upon the Name of Jesus. Jesus became the symbol of their movement and their ideals. As they began to call upon the Lord, He set them free from their bondage and their sins and filled them with His Spirit. The "Jesus People" were born. This movement became the catalyst of the charismatic renewal. This led to a sovereign visitation spanning every denomination in Christendom. It was common to find Lutherans, Methodists, Presbyterians, Catholics, Episcopals and others gathering at city-wide rallies to praise the Name of Jesus. Thousands were converted and set free. Many were healed of diseases; many more received the baptism of the Spirit as on the day of Pentecost, with the evidence of speaking in other tongues. Prayer meetings became the focal point of many churches. For a while the born-again experience made national headlines from coast to coast. It became the topic of newscasts and newspaper articles. Celebrities, politicians and entertainers began to testify of being born again. A few, however, were claiming the experience for acceptance and personal gain. This resulted in weakening the Church's testimony. God only honors those who live what they preach. The fanfare was alive, but there was no force behind it.

Many were discouraged at these events in the charismatic movement and had expected something far better. Remember Elijah? After great spiritual confrontation he flees for his life from wicked Jezebel. In First Kings nineteen he is just about ready to pack it in. God sends an angel and Elijah eats and runs. When he arrives at Horeb, he and God have a church service. This time God is preaching, using illustrated sermons (earthquakes, thunderings, fire, etc.). Elijah thinks he is the only one left in all Israel who is hungry for more of God. But God's records indicated at least 7,000 others! It was at Horeb, the Mount of God, that Elijah received a heavenly perspective on the situation.

We need heavenly perspective. We need to have ears to

hear what the Lord is saying in this hour. God is moving in the hearts of the faithful by power and grace. There was a faithful remnant in Israel that had not bowed the knee to Baal. God had 7,000 He could count on. Seven is the number of perfection. One thousand is a number symbolizing completeness. There was a perfect and complete company of believers that was worshiping the one true God. So it follows that today there is a company of faithful believers willing to follow the Lamb.

Of the 7,000 in Israel, there was one whose name was Elisha. Elisha was God's answer to Elijah's depression. Let's consider the two names and their spiritual significance. *Elijah* means "Yah is God." The ministry of Elijah was a declaration of his name. We see at Carmel a display of the power of the one true God as opposed to the inability of Baal. *Elisha* means "Yah is salvation." We see in the life of Elisha a foreshadowing and unveiling of the universality of the salvation of the Lord in the healing of the king of Syria. Naaman, healed of his leprosy, is a picture of the Gentile nations welcomed into the Covenant under the reign of the King of Kings.

Elijah was to spend the remainder of his days helping Elisha to develop. We are told that when Elijah was commissioned by God to anoint Elisha in his place, he would find him in Abel-meholah (1 Kings 19:16). *Abel-meholah* is translated "meadow of the dance." Dancing is festive and joyous; Abel-meholah is a picture of rejoicing! Paul the apostle tells us to "rejoice evermore" (1 Thess. 5:16); he also exhorts us to "rejoice in the Lord always" (Phil. 4:4). Elisha lived in Abel-meholah. God is looking for people who live in an attitude of rejoicing. We need to allow God to cause us to rejoice in all things. We don't necessarily rejoice *for* all things, but we can rejoice *in* all things. God wants to use a people who express His joy.

I came to the Lord in the early 1970's at the height of the charismatic movement, as did many of my close friends. For many of us, the past several years have been filled with adversity and tribulation. Yet God has been teaching us that we can rejoice in HIM. Even when we "can't see the forest for the trees," we need to rejoice in Him. It is a safeguard for our spirits. Some have had to determine to believe, to "hope against hope" (Rom. 4:18), like Abraham, and rejoice anyway. God is investing in your life through the hardships!

James tells us to "count it all joy" when the going gets tough. God is preparing us for great things. We can't allow ourselves to be fooled by the baals that are worshiped by the unbelieving world. Behind the facade of man-made idols is the sinister spirit of this age. Enduring for the sake of your faith in Christ will reap great reward. The Lord may be allowing certain difficulties to come your way, but like Elisha you can make your home in Abel-meholah. It is there that He will turn your mourning into dancing (Ps. 30:11).

Elisha was *plowing* in a field with twelve pairs of oxen when Elijah met him. (In other words, he was overseeing eleven others.) And he wasn't just giving orders, he was plowing with the twelfth pair. Elisha was plowing and preparing the ground for sowing for his father.

When Jesus was twelve, He went to His Father's house. When His parents found Him, He said He had to be about His Father's work (Luke 2:49). What was Jesus doing? He was plowing the field of his heart and mind to make room for the precious seed of the Word. The Word reaped a perfect harvest in Him, for He was and is the Word. Elisha was plowing, and by example leading eleven others in the same direction.

God has been causing a number of His servants to plow together in preparation for sowing precious seed. They have not been in the forefront where everyone can see them. The public isn't aware of them, but God is. These faithful plowers are part of a team that is pulling together and being faithful to do what their hands find to do. They are serving wholeheartedly in Father's house. They have not "despised the day of small things" (Zech. 4:10), and are believing for greater things in the days ahead. For some, visions and dreams have tarried for a season. We need to be reminded that God is not slow regarding His promises. He will perform what He says. As we plow together in the field, and break up the fallow ground, God will bless our labors and in His time give us what we desire. The words of Habakkuk are timely indeed:

> *Though the fig tree should not blossom,*
> *And there be no fruit on the vines,*
> *Though the yield of the olive should fail,*
> *And the fields produce no food,*
> *Though the flock should be cut off from the fold,*
> *And there be no cattle in the stalls,*
> *Yet I will exult in the Lord,*
> *I will rejoice in the God of my salvation.*
> *The Lord God is my strength,*
> *And He has made my feet like hinds' feet,*
> *And makes me walk on my high places.*

Habakkuk 3:17-19

Chapter Two

Father's House

A nd it came about when the Lord was about to
take up Elijah by a whirlwind to heaven, that
Elijah went with Elisha from Gilgal. And
Elijah said to Elisha, "Stay here please, for the Lord has
sent me as far as Bethel." But Elisha said, "As the Lord
lives and as you yourself live, I will not leave you." So they
went down to Bethel. (2 Kin. 2:1-2)

Elijah is making the final rounds at each place where he has
established ministry. At the outset we notice that both he and
Elisha are at Gilgal. Gilgal has great significance in the redemptive history of Israel and has spiritual significance for our
redemptive history in Christ. *Gilgal* means "circle of stones."
In the Book of Joshua we read that the nation of Israel set up
twelve stones in the midst of the Jordan River and twelve

stones on the dry land as a memorial to the Lord. These were
to remind future generations that the Lord had enabled Israel
to cross the river on dry ground, and also to let them know that
He had "rolled away" the reproach of Egypt. Further, it was at
Gilgal that the Lord instructed Joshua to circumcise all the
males who were born in the wilderness. Circumcision was the
sign of the Abrahamic Covenant. In Genesis chapter seventeen
the Lord speaks the following to Abraham: "This is My covenant, which you shall keep, between Me and you and your
descendants after you: every male among you shall be circumcised...but an uncircumcised male who is not circumcised in
the flesh of his foreskin, that person shall be cut off from his
people; he has broken My covenant..." (v. 10,14)

Under the Old Covenant, circumcision was the initiation
rite into the covenant community. Apart from circumcision
there was no identification with the God of the Covenant. The
circumcision of the men at Gilgal in fulfillment of the condi-
tions of the Abrahamic Covenant foreshadowed the circumcision of our *hearts* in Christ. In Colossians 2:11 Paul tells us:
"...and in Him you were also circumcised with a circumcision
made without hands, in the removal of the body of the flesh by
the circumcision of Christ..." This is a glorious truth. When by
faith we receive and embrace the sacrifice of Christ, there are
a number of things into which we automatically enter. When
Christ, who is the Mediator of the New Covenant in His blood,
sacrificed His life, it was for the redemption of the transgression
that resulted from the first covenant. Through Him we have
received an eternal inheritance. The blessings of a covenant
are only valid when death occurs. This is true today. When a

person bequeaths certain properties in a will, they are not given to the designated party until the person dies. Upon death, however, those designated receive their inheritances.

By the circumcision of Christ we have been translated out of the kingdom of darkness (the reproach of Egypt). The pain of circumcision at Gilgal for the sons of Israel under the Old Covenant cannot be compared to the suffering of Christ on Calvary under the New Covenant. It was here that our sin was exchanged for His righteousness.

Our circumcision occurs at the moment of repentance. When we confess our sinfulness to Christ and accept His substitutionary death, we are born of the Spirit. We begin here at Gilgal, but we don't stop here! On the day of Pentecost Peter said, "Repent and be *baptized*..." (Acts 2:38) While our hearts are circumcised inwardly, water baptism resolves this reality outwardly. The word "baptize" in the Greek means to plunge, dip or immerse. In the Book of Acts the only people who were baptized were those who encountered the Lord Jesus Christ by repentance and confession.

The charismatic renewal saw a large number of people entering into a "Gilgal" experience with the Lord. Many testified of being born again. But the new birth is only the beginning of our salvation! Many who came to Christ in the charismatic movement did not fully understand the Gilgal experience and never progressed beyond that point. How sad for them. Such people remain babes in Christ. They testify of *how* God saved them and *from what* He saved them, but they have never realized *what He saved them for!* Proverbs 29:18 tells us that without a progressive vision, the people live carelessly. Salvation is more than being saved, healed and filled with the Holy Ghost.

Shallow preaching and teaching produces shallow converts. There have been many fine ministries raised up during this era; however, there have also been many individuals who have had little understanding, but have reproduced themselves in the lives of their hearers. We need to be taught from the moment of repentance what God has in store for us.

There has been only ONE purpose, ONE program, and ONE will before the world began in the eternal counsels of the Most High. God's motive is absolutely pure and stems from His love and grace. Some of us in the charismatic movement desperately need our perspectives broadened. Rallying around Gilgal and our conversion experience causes us to emphasize one aspect of the truth to the exclusion of the WHOLE body of truth. Some of God's people seem to give the impression that being saved and having all your prayers answered is all there is. The me-oriented age in which we live has affected much of the preaching we hear. The world does not revolve around me, my denomination or my experience in God. The truth is that all things revolve around Christ and Him alone.

God saves us for fellowship. Christ is the hub around which all things revolve. Without Him at the center we will lose our balance and run off course. To fully appreciate the truth of fellowship with God we must have an understanding of the basic nature of God Himself. It is the Fatherhood of God which is the controlling and ultimate factor that determines His activities in the lives of believers. The Fatherhood of God gives us a PATERNAL OVERSHADOWING and emphasis in all we do. God has intended to have many sons in His one Son, the Lord Jesus Christ. We, as sons, are to share a relationship with the Father of the same kind that Christ shared while He walked the earth. By growing in fellowship with the Father we will grow in service as well. As with the first son He ever created in Eden, God's desire has been to walk in the "cool of the garden" in the midst of the day with each of His sons (Gen. 3:8).

God saves us for service. Gilgal was the place where the oppressive yoke of Egypt was removed. The Lord removes the yoke of sin when we are saved. When that burden of heaviness is lifted from a person, he feels much lighter. However, our lives are still to be yoked! The *Zondervan Pictorial Encyclopedia* tells us that the word "yoke" refers to a heavy wooden frame used to tie two draft animals (such as oxen) together to pull heavy loads such as plows and carts. That doesn't sound exciting, does it?

In Matthew 11:29 Jesus says His yoke is easy and His burden light. He also said if we wanted to have fellowship with Him, we had to get in the yoke! Too many believers have failed to put their heads in the yoke at Gilgal. Servanthood is sharing the yoke with Jesus. What exactly is this yoke? The will of the Father! When God put Adam in the garden, He put him to work. Jesus said, "My food is to do the will of Him who sent Me, and to accomplish His work" (John 4:34).

If we aren't serving God, we are serving ourselves. Whether we realize it or not, we all wear yokes. We are either slaves of sin or slaves of righteousness. The yoke of self, however, leads to slavery and bondage, while the yoke of Jesus leads to liberty and freedom. Let me reiterate that Gilgal is the place of beginnings. If we never fully enter in, we will remain there the rest of our lives. Unfortunately, Christian media actually encourages an attitude of "get all you can." Jesus would not be allowed on certain charismatic talk shows. His message is not "get all you can" — it's "lose all you have"! If we seek to save our lives, we lose them in the final analysis. Jesus was radical! The Christ-centered gospel is a radical gospel. His gospel produces the fruit and supernatural manifestation of the presence of the Kingdom.

Elisha wore the yoke. He was committed. Why Elijah encouraged him to remain at Gilgal is a matter upon which we can only speculate. Perhaps God was perfecting Elisha's faith. Faith is tested; when faith is tested, faith obeys! In Matthew 15:23 Jesus almost disregards the Syrophoenician woman's request for her daughter. Superficially, He seemed cruel. He boldly declared that the children's bread (the blessings of His ministry) was for the house of Israel. He went on to call the Gentiles dogs! She did not despair; she replied humbly that even dogs pick up crumbs that fall from the table. As a result, her faith was rewarded. She received the desire of her heart. Maybe God was allowing a similar thing to happen to Elisha. God was not just going to hand him the ministry on a silver platter; he had to pursue it!

Noting Elisha's example, we should not be satisfied to remain at Gilgal. Not *dis*satisfied (because it is impossible for a child of God to be dissatisfied with the blessing of the Lord), but *unsatisfied.* The taste of good things to come should make us hungry for more. Elisha realized that if he were going to receive all God had for him from Elijah, he had to move on.

When the cloud permeates the meeting in the camp we should rest and abide, but when the cloud lifts we need to move with the cloud. We have heard a great deal about the topic of submission to authority the past several years. Some of this teaching has been good, and some of it very unhealthy. The key to submission is found in the relationship between Elijah and Elisha. It is the ELISHA PRINCIPLE at work. We submit to the anointing! When the anointing lifts through the abuse of authority or sin, and the blessing of the Lord is removed thereby, our submission ends.

Elijah reveals to Elisha that the Lord is sending him to Bethel. He knew it was his time to depart and that the Lord was going to remove him by whirlwind. What he didn't know was where or at what time of day it would happen. It is apparent that God was leading him step by step. Once he obeyed, he received further instruction.

Some of us want to know the end at the beginning of our lives. We want God to show us the whole blueprint before we set out on the journey. There is not one instance in Scripture where God dealt with His people that way, and we cannot assume that He will break the rules for us. We must respond in faith to the light we receive before God gives more light. When Abraham left Ur of the Chaldees he had no idea where he was going, but he knew he had to obey God. If God were to tell us all that He has ordained for us, some of us might shrink away at the revealed will of the Lord. We must walk in the obedience of faith.

Bethel has historical significance. In Genesis chapter twenty-eight Jacob journeys from Haran and decides to camp for the night. He forgot a pillow, so he finds a rock to lay his head on and falls asleep quite readily. (When we place ourselves on the Rock of Ages, we find rest as well!) Jacob dreams he receives a revelation from God. God shows Jacob a ladder reaching to Heaven, and angels ascending to and descending from the presence of the Lord. The Lord then renews the covenant promises He had made to Abraham, committing Himself unconditionally to Jacob. He also assures him of protection and the fulfillment of His promises. As a result, Jacob, upon waking, builds an altar there to the Lord and names the place *Bethel*, meaning "house of God."

The Bethel revelation is so important for the Body of Christ! The apostle Peter tells us that we, the Church, are being built up as a SPIRITUAL HOUSE (Bethel, if you will) for a holy priesthood (1 Pet. 2:5). The writer to the Hebrews tells us that Christ is the Head of His Father's house, and *we* are the house (Heb. 3:6)! The Church is Bethel! We are the temple of the living God! God has purposed to build His house. He placed a wise Master Builder over the construction who was given skilled artisans and craftsmen to oversee the work. When Christ ascended to Heaven He employed apostles, prophets, evangelists, pastors and teachers in the overall blueprint. This is for the purpose of having the house function as effectively and efficiently as possible.

The local church is the visible expression of God's Covenant, because the Church is the covenant community. It is in the local church that the ladder of Christ's presence touches Heaven and releases the blessings of the Father to those in need. It is also a place of development and training. The best seminary in the world is the local church functioning according to the New Testament pattern. Commitment and accountability are essential to growth in the Kingdom. In many circles there has been an unhealthy emphasis on personalities and ministries, which has produced followers of men rather than followers of God. As a result, many take the words of these men as infallible without searching the Scripture for themselves. Paul struggled with the church at Corinth over this very issue. All the gifts were in operation, and supernatural manifestations were commonplace, but some were of Apollos, others believed Peter, and still others were convinced that to be really "mature" you had to follow Paul. "Has Christ been divided?" Paul asks (1 Cor. 3:1-ff). How grievous this is to the Lord. Many ministries which once were used mightily of God are no longer in the forefront. They began to believe all the press releases about themselves. As a result God lifted the anointing.

If we seek to obtain a following and promote our own ministries, we end up building our kingdoms instead of the Kingdom of God. Many of those same ministries experienced casualties as well. Men and women of God who were highly accredited fell into sin. Many of their followers stumbled and fell. Brethren, these things ought not be. God is wanting to do a great thing in the earth. Let's learn from our mistakes. We need to stop making gods of mere men, and let God be God.

In the New Testament, especially the Book of Acts, we notice that when people were converted, they were PLACED by God in fellowship with other believers in a local church. God's pattern has not changed. If we desire the power we read of in the Book of Acts we need to follow the pattern revealed there. Some have wandered for years without being enfolded into a local church. Like lone rangers they wander from city to city and town to town, never being grafted in. Their problems stem back to Gilgal, where they forgot to stick their heads in the yoke with Jesus. Waiting until they find the "perfect church," they themselves fail to see their own imperfections and rebellion. The thought of allowing God to smooth rough edges in the fire of fellowship with other imperfect people is repulsive to them. They will never come to know what it is to be transformed into the image of Christ.

Others fail to get "plugged in" because they are just plain lazy. It may be too hard to get out of bed on Sunday morning. These same dear people, however, are continually seeking private counsel to help them overcome their problems. I have decided that if a person wants my counsel, he must sit through at least two consecutive weeks of my preaching. Those that make the effort really absorb the preached Word, and their problems are solved without having to call me back!

I find it interesting that the charismatic movement has produced such a multitude of overnight counselors. Everybody specializes in some form of counsel. I am not "knocking" these areas of "specialization." I have seen much good accomplished by inner healing ministries, deliverance, and self-image therapy. But I have also seen quite a bit of error. We need to come back to the foundation of the house. The local church, when it functions as it should, will minister to all the needs of God's people. If this is not happening, the leadership is failing to provide the necessary equipping or the believers are immature and rebellious. The charismatic movement tends to elevate the personal ministry of individuals and leave the local church on the periphery.

But be of good cheer! The Spirit of God has been stirring the local church. The proper emphasis is being restored. The local church is to be the center for renewal, revival and restoration in the lives of God's people. Many large parachurch organizations have been folding because support has been down. I believe people are beginning to realize that our major support should be given to the local church. This is not to say that all parachurch organizations are unbiblical. Some have done a tremendous work for God where the Church has failed to meet a need. But a parachurch organization is not an end in itself — it is a feeder program back to the local church. God never called one-man- or one-woman-ministries to win the world for Jesus. Many of God's people are believing the wrong things and are motivated to give through guilt or impulse. These people believe they are being prompted by the Spirit of God.

God isn't committed to building our kingdoms, He is committed to building His. We need to lay our kingdoms at His feet. It is His house that He has chosen to indwell. He is building a mighty army of flesh and blood believers functioning according to the proper working of each individual part (Eph. 4:11). The foundation of the house is the Rock on which Jacob slept: Christ and Christ alone. In Revelation 21:22-24 we have a picture of the Church in all her glory! "And I saw no temple in it, for the Lord God, the Almighty, and the Lamb, are its temple. And the city has no need of the sun or of the moon to shine upon it, for the glory of God has illumined it, and its lamp is the Lamb" (v. 22, 23). What is the Spirit revealing to us about the Church in these verses? A temple is a man-made structure; the Church is not, but is a holy temple conceived in the mind of God before the world began. Man cannot construct a dwelling place for the Lord. Heaven is His throne and the earth His footstool. Nothing we construct could possibly contain Him. But He has brought forth a Church through the finished work of Christ. That Church is intended by God to contain the manifold grace of God in its expression.

The sun and moon are the natural luminaries with which God has lit the world in which we live. In God's spiritual house there is no room for natural light. Natural methods do not produce supernatural results. If you begin in the flesh, you end up with...flesh! If unbelievers are attracted to anything other than the light of Christ, we are failing to be reflectors of His light. As the moon is a reflector of the sun, so are we to shine with the brightness of Christ's glory, reflecting His radiance in the midst of the darkness of this world. We are the light of the world (Matt. 5:14). "The path of the righteous is like the light of dawn, that shines brighter and brighter until the full day" (Prov. 4:18)!

In the days ahead I believe God desires to move in a greater way to bring a fuller manifestation of the glory of His presence. An old Pentecostal chorus expresses this thought well:

> *There's a mighty glory coming,*
> *And it's coming down today,*
> *And it's coming here to stay,*
> *There's a mighty glory coming,*
> *And it's coming from the presence*
> *of the Lord!*

Just as Elisha was determined to follow Elijah to Bethel, so we must embrace the Bethel revelation and move on with God. The local church is where it's happening in the days ahead. Let's be sure we are plugged in and functioning as we should for the glory of God!

Chapter Three

We Are Standing on Holy Ground

*T*hen the sons of the prophets who were at Bethel came out to Elisha and said to him, *"Do you know that the Lord will take away your master from over you today?" And he said, "Yes, I know; be still!" And Elijah said to him, "Elisha, please stay here, for the Lord has sent me to Jericho." But he said, "As the Lord lives, and as you yourself live, I will not leave you." So they came to Jericho.* (2 Kin. 2:3-4)

In the early history of the prophetic ministry of Israel, "schools of the prophets" or "sons of the prophets" evolved. The term does not give us an accurate definition. The earliest mention of such groups is found in the first Book of Samuel. One might think Samuel started these schools for the development of future prophets. This is not true. Historical records reveal that these men were followers of the prophets who did nothing more than act as a support group. They were men who wanted to be a part of what was happening. In the biblical record we have no indication that God ever called any of His prophets from among these men. The call of God to the prophetic office was by sovereign election. These men posed a definite problem for Elisha. They were always getting in the way! By way of example, they typify a common malady in the Body of Christ.

A number of believers in the charismatic scheme of things are always looking for the latest revelation or the newest truth. Sadly, many of these individuals are learning but never come to a knowledge of the truth. They are carried along by every wind of doctrine. Always looking for the "deep things of God," their lives are marked by shallowness. By the time they ought to be teachers, they themselves need to be taught the elementary oracles of God.

Word got around that Elijah would be removed. The sons of the prophets had probably heard it from Elijah himself. Rumors spread.

Elisha's response to these characters was far from amiable. He was obviously not impressed with them. There will always be those who will endeavor to hold you back. Afraid to move out in unknown areas themselves, they think it their duty to discourage others from going any further than they have. Their arguments for not moving on are usually excuses for their own personal insecurities. This does not just happen in the pews of the church, this happens from the pulpit as well. Preachers who are afraid of the moving of God's Spirit often quench the Spirit from moving at all. They play God, thus preventing their congregations from moving into greater freedom. They work overtime to make sure nothing gets too "out of hand." The Kingdom will always manifest itself with power. Everywhere Jesus went people were healed, delivered and set free. Some of them made quite a bit of noise and got excited. Preachers afraid of a move of God are appreciative when He moves elsewhere. The only cure for this fear is honest self-examination in the presence of the Lord.

The Word of God is not void of power, but we can make it appear that way. Without the Spirit, the Word is lifeless. We need to learn how to appraise things by the Spirit of God. He abides within us and shall lead us into all truth. The sons of the prophets were void of spiritual depth and understanding — they were trying to hold Elisha back from doing what he knew he must do. He was extreme and fanatical in their eyes. They justified their words by appearing to embrace Elisha's best interests. "Don't you know your master is going to be taken from over you today?" they asked. "Aren't you going a bit too far with this thing, Elisha? Don't you know you will only be hurt in the end?" Of course Elisha wasn't being foolish or presumptuous. He had counted the cost. Elisha responded by telling them to mind their own business. They couldn't discern his motives. They couldn't even see past their own noses, let alone understand his heart motive.

Elisha was driven by an inward desire for a deeper revelation of God. It was a consuming passion. It was his "magnificent obsession." Even Elijah couldn't persuade Elisha to tarry at Bethel. He must, yes *must*, go on!

To reiterate, Bethel is the place of commitment and accountability. It is the house of God; the Church. We have stressed the importance of being enfolded into a local expression of the Body of Christ.

It is not enough, however, to merely be on the membership list of a local church and to tithe. It isn't even enough to be present at all the meetings. There are those in this hour who are PLAYING church instead of BEING the Church. They become permanent fixtures; permanent and immovable. "Playing church" is the reason the Body of Christ is so pathetically weak in some areas. The house of God is more than a social club. It is the Body of Christ, and is to be the fulness of Him who fills all in all. We cannot be content to remain with the sons of the prophets at Bethel when God is calling us further. As Elisha, we need to see beyond the outward appearance of religion and a "religious" life-style. We must determine to fulfill our ministry one to another as God intended us to.

The purpose of the five-fold ministries of the Church (Eph. 4:11) is to equip the saints for the work of service (v. 12). The Body is a living organism. It is attached to a living Head, and He is ordering all things after the counsel of His will.

As a living organism, the Body is to function according to the proper working of each individual part. If our feet cannot move, we are not going anywhere; if our liver does not function, it won't be long before a toxic condition sets in and leads to death. When the Lord saves us and places us in His Church, we are to function in our particular capacity. The prophet Amos has a fitting word (6:1): "Woe to those who are at ease in Zion"! It is so easy to become comfortable and complacent in the Church. We need to shake ourselves and become loosed from our captivity (Is. 52:1, 2)!

God has called us to follow Elijah to Jericho. There are battles to be fought and strongholds to be taken. Since it is easier not to confront the enemy, we could remain at Bethel. But if we want all that God has, we must press on to Jericho (even if Elijah tries to persuade us otherwise)!

Jericho has tremendous significance.

In the Book of Joshua, chapter five, Joshua has an encounter with an individual whom the Scriptures refer to as the "Captain of the host of the Lord." This was a theophany; theologians use this term to describe an appearance of the Son of God before He became human flesh. Why should Joshua encounter the Captain of the Hosts of Heaven? Why is he wearing military apparel? War? "But God gave us this land! You mean we have to fight for it?" Psalm 24:8 reminds us that the Lord is a warrior. The individual Joshua encountered not only wanted to know if Joshua was on His side, but had a drawn sword in His hand to encourage a proper decision. Joshua was commanded to remove his sandals because he was on holy ground. The Captain gave him detailed instruction concerning how the sons of Israel were to capture Jericho. Jericho was the first city in the Promised Land to be conquered by Israel under the leadership of Joshua. Isn't it fascinating that no weapons were used to demolish the walls of Jericho? What kind of army would march around a city once a day for six days, seven times on the seventh day, and merely shout the walls down? God's army! Can you imagine the perplexity of the men of Jericho as they watched the sons of Israel? I'm sure the men of the city got dizzy. On the seventh day, after the seventh time around, the Israelites shouted and "the walls came tumblin' down!" At Jericho the sons of Israel were receiving an object lesson from the Lord. If they were to possess the land, they had to follow the Lord's strategy. This would lead to absolute victory.

The charismatic movement had experienced a wonderful rekindling of the truths represented by Jericho. *Jericho* means "fragrance." Fragrance reminds me of the altar of incense in the tabernacle of Moses and the heavenly tabernacle (Ex. 30:1-10; Rev. 8:3). The incense symbolizes praise, prayer and worship. In the tabernacle of Moses, the incense passed through the thin veil concealing the Ark of the Covenant and ascended above the Mercy Seat to the Shekinah cloud. It was a "soothing fragrance" before the Lord. The angel in Revelation chapter eight also holds a vial of incense, representing the prayers and worship of the saints. What does this have to do with warfare? Everything! The Christian life is one of battle. Paul tells us that it is not an earthly battle, but a spiritual one. In Ephesians 6:12 he states, "We wrestle not against flesh and blood, but against principalities, against powers..." (KJV) Since our warfare is spiritual, our weapons and strategy must be spiritual as well. "Our weapons are not carnal, but mighty through God to the pulling down of..." the walls of Jericho (2 Cor. 10:3-5, KJV).

One of the most exciting aspects of the charismatic movement has been the teaching on praise, worship and warfare.

The lifting of hands, singing in the Spirit, singing of Scripture, spontaneous praise and applause are acceptable responses to the presence of the Lord. The battle of Jericho began when Joshua worshiped the Captain of the Lord of Hosts the night before it all began. One of the most exciting pictures of worship and warfare is found in Psalm 110:3:

> *Thy people will volunteer freely*
> *in the day of Thy power;*
> *In holy array, from the womb of the dawn,*
> *Thy youth are to Thee as the dew.*

The battle of Jericho was won by the shout of praise! If you read the remainder of Revelation 8:3, you discover that after the angel pours out the incense before the throne, great thunderings begin and the wrath and judgment of God upon the ungodly follows. The call of Jericho is a call to aggressive spiritual warfare. This kind of warfare begins with worship and ends with worship. In our battles against the forces of darkness we dare not rush in where angels fear to tread. First we must come into the presence of our heavenly Captain and worship in the beauty of holiness. It is in His presence that we receive our directives and strategies. Praise, worship, prayer and intercession are our spiritual weapons. Psalm 149:6-9 says:

> *Let the high praises of God be in their mouth,*
> *And a two-edged sword in their hand* [the Word],
> *To execute vengeance on the nations,*
> *And punishment on the peoples;*
> *To bind their kings with chains,*

And their nobles with fetters of iron;
To execute on them the judgment written;
This is an honor for all His godly ones.
Praise the Lord!

What an encouragement to be praising people! Praise accomplishes great things in the realm of the Spirit. Praise and intercession are mighty weapons to be used in aggressive conflict with the forces of darkness that hinder the moving of God's Spirit. A praising people is a powerful people. When we apply principles of aggressive spiritual warfare we will give birth to restoration and revival. Jesus said the gates of hell would not prevail against the onslaught of the Church. In Isaiah 53:12 the Spirit of the Lord declares that Christ will divide the spoils of battle among the strong. Paul admonishes us to be STRONG in the Lord (Eph. 6:10).

Praise is the highest expression of faith we can render to God in the face of spiritual onslaught. Praise is reliance on the strength of God, not on my own abilities. Apart from Him I am no match for the enemy. My motive in praising has nothing to do with feelings. I praise Him because He is worthy!

"Worthy is the Lamb...to receive power and riches and wisdom and might and honor and glory and blessing" (Rev. 5:12)! Praise releases the presence of God. In Psalm 97:5 we are reminded that "the mountains melted like wax at the presence of the Lord"! As we praise Him in the great congregation, His very presence is what causes mountains of satanic oppression to be removed. "Let God arise, let His enemies be scattered..." cries the psalmist (Ps. 68:1). Jericho, the place of absolute victory, was won as a result of surrender, worship and praise. We need to move from Bethel to Jericho!

While these truths have been shared repeatedly by many great men and women of God in the charismatic movement, there is more to be learned. We need to be willing to be taught from the Word by the Spirit of the Lord. The days ahead will be marked by greater expressions of celebration in the presence of the Lord. Praise and worship are keys to functioning in the supernatural. New wine requires new wineskins. Let's allow God to do a work in our hearts and to enlarge our understanding in the days that lie ahead. In the words of Bonnie Low:

> *The Lord is marching on,*
> *And His army is ever strong.*
> *And His glory shall be seen upon our land!*
> *Raise the anthem, sing the Victor's song,*
> *Praise the Lord, for the battle's won!*
> *No weapon formed against us shall stand!*
> *For the Captain of the Hosts is Jesus,*
> *We're following in His footsteps.*
> *No foe can stand against us in the fray.*
> *We are marching in Messiah's band,*
> *The keys of victory in His mighty Hand!*
> *Let us march on to take our Promised Land!*

Chapter Four

Roll, Jordan, Roll!

*A*nd the sons of the prophets who were at Jericho approached Elisha and said to him, "Do you know that the Lord will take away your master from over you today?" And he answered, "Yes, I know; be still." Then Elijah said to him, "Please stay here, for the Lord has sent me to the Jordan." And he said, "As the Lord lives, and as you yourself live, I will not leave you." So the two of them went on. (2 Kin. 2:5-6)*

Every phase of growth in the truth and every progressive development in our lives by the Spirit of God causes us to appreciate that which has gone before. We do not always understand why the Lord leads us in a certain pathway, but once we arrive at our destination our eyes are opened. Each

successive step we take into the things of God is built upon
what has gone before. We have seen that we must proceed
from Gilgal to Bethel, and ultimately to Jericho. We have seen
that circumcision leads to commitment and accountability, and
commitment and accountability to warfare. Not with each
other, as the enemy would have us think, but with evil spirits.

Somewhere in our journey God calls us eastward to the
Jordan. The Jordan was further east than Gilgal. (East is always
the place of beginning in the Scriptures.) Judah, the leading
tribe of Israel, camped at the eastern end of the tabernacle
(Num. 2:3). Why would God call Elijah to go backward? In
the Kingdom of God, sometimes we must go backward in
order to go forward. The way to exaltation is humility.

Elisha has been clinging to Elijah all morning. They began
their journey at Gilgal, and probably by mid-morning arrived
at Bethel. After leaving Bethel, they made a trek to Jericho.
They had walked at least fifteen miles by this time. It could be
late afternoon by now. A dip in the Jordan, as muddy as it is,
might have been rather refreshing and welcome at this point.

Elisha's heart burns for more than he presently has. The
sons of the prophets have no empathy for the depths that he
desires to explore. In certain charismatic circles, different ones
have made Jericho their home. They are beyond Bethel and
sing, enjoy praise and celebrate wholeheartedly. They might
even dance on occasion. They seem to understand spiritual
warfare and appear to have the faith that moves mountains.
Perhaps they do! They read all the latest Christian books,
subscribe to a few Christian magazines and have 24-hour

Christian programming on their local cable networks. But something is missing from their lives. What has gone wrong? In Revelation two John writes a letter on behalf of the Lord Jesus to the church at Ephesus. Within two years after this church was established it grew to 40,000 members. Their doctrines were correct; their standards were high. But Jesus was disappointed with them. Why? Because they left their first love. They reduced everything to a set of rules and regulations. Not unlike those at Bethel, the problem is this: they had developed Christian "professionalism." They meant well, but they missed the mark.

Before we judge too harshly, let's look at our own lives. These pitfalls are subtle and dangerous. None of us are exempt from the wiles of the enemy. The church at Ephesus had been so well fed that they believed they had "arrived." They failed to discern intellectualism from outworking in the heart. The message must not only be woven into our minds, it must be woven into our hearts. The charismatic movement has imparted great truths to multitudes. Unfortunately, many of these have not been allowed to take root. Once upon a time in the wilderness, a man named Moses had a similar problem. Listen to the sermon he preached one morning: "But Jeshurun grew fat and kicked — You are grown fat, thick, and sleek — Then he forsook God who made him, And scorned the Rock of his salvation" (Deut. 32:15). Some of us have become spiritual gluttons! Connoisseurs of the finest in doctrinal exposition, we sample here and there until our minds are full. We develop fat heads and lean hearts.

God declared that this kind of spiritual gluttony had led to a scornful attitude in the sons of Israel. When we grow fat we kick and complain. We scorn the Rock of our salvation. We need to learn how to hunger and thirst after righteousness all over again. What does Jesus say to those who are so "well-fed"? He says, "I have food to eat that you do not know about" (John 4:32). Scripture tells us that strong meat belongs to the mature. Jesus goes on to tell us what strong meat really is: "My food is to do the will of Him who sent Me..." (John 4:34) Doing the will of the Father is the strong meat! The Word commands and demands absolute surrender and obedience to the Word of God. In the days ahead we need to hear the truth of absolute obedience to the Lordship of Jesus Christ again and again. If we want all that God intends for us, we cannot be content to remain at Jericho. We must go on to the Jordan. *Jordan* means "the descender"; it is a picture of death. We will follow Elijah and Elisha to the Jordan. Burial at sea, anyone...?

Chapter Five

Crossing Over on Dry Ground!

*N*ow fifty men of the sons of the prophets went and stood opposite them at a distance, while the two of them stood by the Jordan. And Elijah took his mantle and folded it together and struck the waters, and they were divided here and there, so that the two of them crossed over on dry ground. (2 Kin. 2:7-8)

The Jordan is the one place to which the sons of the prophets won't tag along. At best they can only watch from a distance. The sons of the prophets are lookers, not takers. Jordan, "the descender," is a picture of death and transition. Elijah was being escorted to Heaven beyond the Jordan, while Elisha was leaving his ministry to the man of God.

Do you remember what happened when the sons of Israel

came to the banks of the Jordan? It was then that Joshua was commanded to sanction the priests to carry the Ark 2,000 cubits ahead of the camp of Israel into the muddy waters (Josh. 3:4). This symbolized to the people that God was going before them to make a way. He would bring them into the land of Canaan. God always goes before His people. He is consistent in all His ways. The Ark would enter the Jordan before the Israelites. Because of the Ark of the Covenant, the Jordan parted. The Ark symbolizes the fulness of the Godhead.

We know that fulness was and is contained in the Lord Jesus Christ. When He began His earthly ministry, He too entered Jordan's waters to be baptized, in order to fulfill all righteousness. Baptism is symbolic of death and resurrection. That act of obedience in the life of Christ caused the heavens to be opened, the Spirit to descend upon Him, and the Father to utter these words: "Thou art My Beloved Son, in Thee I am well-pleased" (Luke 3:22). This captured the essence of the entire life of the Lord Jesus. He ultimately tasted death for every man. He entered into the waters of death not only symbolically, but literally:

> *...although He existed in the form of God, [He] did not regard equality with God a thing to be grasped, but emptied Himself, taking the form of a bond-servant, and being made in the likeness of men. And being found in appearance as a man, He humbled Himself by becoming obedient to the point of death, even death on a cross.* (Phil. 2:6-8)

From the beginning of His public ministry, Jesus lived the principle revealed in symbolic Jordan. Death to self-will is the

Jordan's message. When we read of Jesus' struggle in the Garden of Gethsemane, we wonder if He was wavering. In Matthew chapter four, we see that Jesus had already made His choice. His struggle in Gethsemane was merely the outworking of His wilderness experience. His meat was to do the Father's will, regardless of the cost.

One may then question the validity of Gilgal. Wasn't Christ's death what brought me to Gilgal? Why was Jordan necessary if all was done for me? While it is true that Gilgal is where I realize that Christ died FOR me, it is also where I must realize that Christ died AS me. In other words, when Christ died, I died! He took the punishment I deserved. But Christ's death goes beyond the Gilgal experience. It isn't until we arrive at Jordan that we understand that Christ's death must be effective IN me! While His work on Calvary has imparted new life and righteousness and freed me from condemnation, living out that new life takes a series of daily choices. Sanctification is a process that takes all our lives. God's grace has saved me, and His grace will sanctify me. Grace is the Divine enablement to fulfill the will of the Father and negate the will of self. Grace is God's power to apply the death of Christ to my everyday life and for me to be transformed into Christ's image as a result. Paul prays for this in Philippians 3:10-11: "That I may know Him [as Elisha knew Him], and the power of His resurrection and the fellowship of His sufferings [the Jordan], being conformed to His death; in order that I may attain to the resurrection from the dead."

A babe in Christ (one having the Gilgal revelation) cannot

handle the full intention of the cross. Surely he can appreciate that old things are passing away, but becoming new takes numerous choices over the span of a lifetime. Repentance is both a single act and a lifetime walk. Young converts are being carried and cuddled by the Father. They are babes. They thrive on milk. Problems come when babes who should be ready for meat still prefer to have milk. Like the sons of the prophets, they'll go so far and no farther. But what about the hidden things, those things we hide in our hearts that we don't want to get rid of?

I used to have a junk closet where I kept things that had sentimental value. Year after year more would pile up. I never used any of the items in the closet, but I couldn't bear to part with them. I brought them with me when I got married. My wife had no sentimental attachments to my "junk," so she conveniently disposed of it. Our relationship with Jesus works the same way. We were married to sin before we met Christ, but after we met Him we changed partners. He then began to clean out the closets! In Psalm 90:8 the psalmist reminds us that God allows His light to shine on our "secret sins" when we come into His presence.

Without a doubt we can rejoice in the Gilgal experience and sing "He took my sins away". And we can see the need to have the security of Bethel's revelation. We enjoy the fellowship of the caring community. We even get excited about winning some victories for the Kingdom by marching around Jericho with the army of the Lord! But the Jordan is different. It is easier to stand off at a distance with the sons of the prophets because the Jordan experience is something each of us must face alone. The Jordan becomes the place where God gets very personal. He gets very particular with us in the Jordan. It is here that the deathblow is given to those things we secretly admire as much as or more than God Himself. Some of those things come in religious packages. They might be ambitions that are carnal and run contrary to the nature and character of Christ. The Surgeon's knife may cut through the motives behind our goals. It may expose our constant scheming to have things work out "our way" all the time. The Jordan experience may reveal the political games we try to play with our church board, or the backbiting we conceal behind our smooth talk or the unforgiving spirit we harbor toward those who have offended us. The heavenly Surgeon uses a double-edged sword! If it hurts, we need to take heed and make some changes.

For the word of God is living and active and sharper than any two-edged sword, and piercing as far as the division of soul and spirit, of both joints and marrow, and able to judge the thoughts and intentions of the heart. (Heb. 4:12)

Some of our "good works" are not so good in the eyes of God because our motives are impure. Many of us want a deeper walk with God. We pray, "God, do a deep work in me." We want to be used mightily of God. We want the supernatural to be manifest in our lives. God takes us at our word and gives us what we ask for. The problem is that sometimes we don't realize what we're asking for! If we want all God has, He will lead us to the Jordan. It's at Jordan that sin is exposed at its roots.

Do you not know that all of us who have been baptized into Christ Jesus have been baptized into His death? (Rom. 6:3)

The Jordan will cost us everything. Many have been overwhelmed with the baptism and gift of the Holy Spirit. But it is only the doorway. Multitudes have had the Pentecostal experience during the charismatic renewal, but have desired the power without the PERSON. The Person is the Power! You can't have the gifts without the Giver. And the Giver is a Person! That Person is the Holy Spirit of God, and He is holy! There has been a lack of emphasis on holiness, but God is raising up a standard for holiness!

When John the Baptist spoke of Jesus' ministry, he declared:

As for me, I baptize you with water for repentance, but He who is coming after me is mightier than I...He will baptize you with the Holy Spirit and fire. (Matt. 3:11)

When we receive the Holy Spirit, we get the fire. You can't have the one without the other. Isaiah asks the following question:

Who among us can live with the consuming fire? Who among us can live with continual burning? (Is. 33:14b)

If we relegate these verses to a place of speaking only of the fires of hell, we miss their import for the present time. To live in God's presence is to live in the fire. He baptizes us in fire. The fire is present to consume the dross and refine the gold. The gold is the perfecting of the image of Christ in our lives.

This is the deeper life. As we come face to face with God and behold Him in all His glory, the fire of His presence stirs up the impurities in our hearts (the dross) and brings them to the surface. He desires to skim them off in order to purify the gold. Paul puts it this way:

> *But we all, with unveiled face beholding as in a mirror the glory of the Lord, are being transformed into the same image from glory to glory, just as from the Lord, the Spirit. (2 Cor. 3:18)*

This is the message of the Jordan. I believe with all my heart that the days ahead will be marked by a return to the apostolic preaching of the cross. God is calling us more than ever in this hour to come to the Jordan. There is new life in the waters of death. Isaiah explains who can live in the fire:

> *He who walks righteously,*
> *And speaks with sincerity,*
> *He who rejects unjust gain,*
> *And shakes his hands so that they hold no bribe;*
> *He who stops his ears from hearing about bloodshed,*
> *And shuts his eyes from looking upon evil;*
> *He will dwell on the heights;*
> *His refuge will be the impregnable rock;*
> *His bread will be given him;*
> *His water will be sure.* (Is. 33:15-16)

The fire is the agent of God to purify our characters. The more we allow the fire to consume the dross, the more precious gold and silver will be revealed; and greater power of God will be released through us. This needs to happen both individually and corporately. Once we learn to respond properly to the fire, it becomes the light in our hearts that burns brighter and brighter. Godly zeal is a great motivational force that will drive the Church to sublime heights of glory! We need to be able to say with Christ: "Zeal for Thy house will consume Me" (Ps. 69:9; John 2:17).

It is time to cast off the fear of change. Rather than stand at a distance from Jordan, we should go right to the edge of its banks with Elisha and allow God to move in all His fulness in our lives! David prophesies these words:

Thy people shall be WILLING in the day of Thy power. (Ps. 110:3, KJV)

Our willingness will cause the waters to part and we will cross over Jordan on dry ground. The mantle which Elijah used to strike the waters speaks of the finished work of Christ. When we reckon ourselves dead to sin and alive to God, we find that sin no longer dominates our lives. When Jesus cried "It is finished" (John 19:30), He condemned sin in the flesh. He nullified it as a principle that would enslave us. The cross has greater power than sin! There we become "more than conquerors" in Christ. Those who stand at a distance from the Jordan never experience the fulness of God's grace. Those who are willing to fellowship with Christ in His sufferings will enter into resurrection life! It is not until we stand on resurrection ground that we can ask what we will of the Father and have it done for us (John 15:7). Glory to God! For Elisha the best was yet to come! In the words of Jesus:

Arise, let us go from here! (John 14:31)

Chapter Six

What Do You Want?

*N**ow it came about when they had crossed over, that Elijah said to Elisha, "Ask what I shall do for you before I am taken from you." And Elisha said, "Please, let a double portion of your spirit be upon me." And he said, "You have asked a hard thing. Nevertheless, if you see me when I am taken from you, it shall be so for you; but if not, it shall not be so."*
(2 Kin. 2:9-10)

When two people are serious about one another they usually can't see enough of each other. They seem inseparable. After a reasonable length of time the young lady begins to anticipate Prince Charming's popping the question. She has rehearsed her answer thousands of times in her mind before the final moment. She can't wait! Finally the day arrives, and she feels all warm and tingly inside because she's ready! When that incredible dream you've been waiting for becomes a reality, you get excited, too!

Elisha was no different. He knew what he wanted. Some of us never receive answers to our prayers because we don't know what we want, or are just plain afraid to ask. Not Elisha! He knew exactly what he wanted and was determined to get a shot at his dreams. Consider for a moment what has transpired until now: Elisha has clung to Elijah like a leech even when Elijah requested that he leave him alone. (Nevertheless, Elijah doesn't seem to be upset with his disciple. In all actuality, God had already informed Elijah of His plans for Elisha.) What would you do if someone kept following you around? Find out what the person wanted, right? Elijah wants to hear it from Elisha's lips. Without a doubt the aged prophet knew full well what his replacement desired.

If we never verbalize our desires, they may never material-ize. Jesus said that we could have whatever we *say*, not what we *think*! (Mark 11:23) "Elisha, what do you want?" Elijah asked. "I want a double portion of what you have!" came the reply. What was he really asking for? Look at Deuteronomy 21:17:

> *But he shall acknowledge the first-born ... by giving him a double portion of all that he has, for he is the beginning of his strength; to him belongs the right of the first-born.*

Elisha wanted the rights of the firstborn son! Elijah had no sons, at least none that we know of. Nevertheless, Elisha was his son in the faith, as Timothy was to Paul. The firstborn had the birthright. The ultimate fulfillment of the right of the first-born is Jesus Himself. In Hebrews 1:6-9 we are told:

And when He again brings the first-born into the world, He says, "And let all the angels of God worship Him"...of the Son He says, "Thy throne, O God, is forever and ever, And the righteous scepter is the scepter of His kingdom. Thou hast loved righteousness and hated lawlessness; Therefore God, Thy God, hath anointed Thee with the oil of gladness ABOVE Thy companions."

Jesus Christ has preeminence over all the works of His hands. He is our Elder Brother and our Sovereign Lord. Elisha was asking for the right to inherit all that Elijah had. This was a spiritual inheritance. The double portion was the very author-ity and prophetic mantle in which Elijah walked. Quite a re-quest! God approves of big dreams. God specializes in doing the impossible. What are we believing God for in this era? Now that the charismatic tide has risen and waned, are we going to believe for greater things or give it all over to the devil and wait for the rapture? I believe God has more...much more! And I believe He wants us to ask Him for it; ask, seek, and knock. We need to believe God for an outpouring of the Spirit that will outshine and outdo anything we have thus far experienced. We need to believe for great victory! The people who dwell in darkness already are convinced that doom is on the horizon. The threat of nuclear annihilation looms over our youth. The threat of a lack of natural resources has driven some to horde supplies. Should we, the Church, the light of the world and the salt of the earth, preach the same pessimistic message? We have the ANSWER: *Christ* is the Hope of glory! Before we consign planet earth over to the antichrist and the hosts of hell, we should be storming Heaven for a rain of glory. The prophet of old said, "Ask for rain in the time of the latter rain" (see Zech. 10:1).

Zechariah was saying, "Don't just ask for a drizzle, ask for a torrential downpour!" All things that Christ has are available to the Church. The double portion is available to the many sons in the one Son. I believe the Lord is giving the Church an invitation in this hour, the same one Elijah gave Elisha: "Ask what I shall do for you..." Our response can turn the tide of history!

Chapter Seven

Having a Single Eye!

*T*hen it came about as they were going along and talking, that behold, there appeared a chariot of fire and horses of fire which separated the two of them. And Elijah went up by a whirlwind to heaven. And Elisha saw it and cried out, "My father, my father, the chariots of Israel and its horsemen!" And he saw him no more.(2 Kin. 2:11-12a)

Nothing worth having ever comes easy. The desires long harbored in the recesses of our beings are worth paying a price for. Elijah put a condition on Elisha's request: "If you see me when I go..." It wasn't enough for Elisha to cling to his master from city to city; now he had to glue his eyes to him and not let him out of his sight!

Singleness of eye is a rare commodity in the Kingdom.

Jesus said that the lamp of the body is the *eye*. When our eyes
are single (clear), our whole beings are resplendent with light.
When our eyes are not single (indicating a divided heart), our
whole being is darkened (Luke 11:34). Paul exhorts the believers at Colossae to "set [their] mind on things above" (Col.
3:2). We are to look at Jesus and fix our gaze upon Him if our
faith is to be perfected (Heb. 12:2). Our eyes need to be riveted
to the One who occupies the throne! Some have placed all
their faith in the teachings of men, the methods of men, the
precepts of men. True faith is fastened to the Lord Jesus Christ.
He is the Head over all things for the sake of the Church.
Church growth principles are good and have their place, but
"success" doesn't necessarily indicate that a real touch of the
Divine is in the midst. We need to have the singleness of
purpose that the Godhead shares if we are to see God's best in
the Church. In Ephesians 1:9-10 Paul reveals the ultimate
intention of the Father's eternal purposes:

> *He made known to us the mystery of His will, according to
> His kind intention which He purposed in Him with A VIEW
> TO AN ADMINISTRATION SUITABLE TO THE FUL-
> NESS OF THE TIMES, THAT IS, THE SUMMING UP
> OF ALL THINGS IN CHRIST, things in the heavens and
> things upon the earth.*

God has His eyes on one thing. All things are to be summed
up in Christ. He is to be the center of all our activities. The
manifest presence of Christ is the crowning glory of the Church.
If we are to receive a double portion as Elisha, our eyes need to

be directed toward Christ. There is one will in Heaven. There should be one will on Earth as well. The eye is only a mirror of the spirit. If our eyes are not single and intent on one purpose, it means our hearts are divided. James had a strong warning for the early Church in this regard:

Draw near to God and He will draw near to you. Cleanse your hands, you sinners; and purify your hearts, you DOUBLE-MINDED. (James 4:8)

We need to keep our eyes on what the Lord is doing and follow Him. One recurring phrase that the Lord Jesus used in the gospels and in the Book of Revelation is, "He who has an ear, let him hear what the Spirit says to the churches."

We live in an age when many things prevent our eyes from being "single." These can occupy our time and keep us from sitting at Jesus' feet. Rightly did Elijah say to Elisha "...you have asked a hard thing..." There is so much to preoccupy us that we can go for weeks without evaluating our personal walks with God. Entertainment, various media, new electronics, computers; we live in an age of advancing technology and power. But man's power cannot compare to the power of the Lord. We need to return to seeking God. His promise is still as valid as the day He spoke it to Jeremiah:

Thus says the Lord who made the earth, the Lord who formed it to establish it, the Lord is His name, "Call to Me, and I will answer you, and I will tell you great and mighty things, which you do not know." (Jer. 33:2-3)

Chapter thirty-three of Jeremiah is a promise of revival and restoration. Elijah and Elisha are immersed in fellowship when there is an angelic visitation and Elijah is borne to Heaven in a chariot. Only one other man in the Old Testament simply "disappeared" into Heaven: Enoch. East of the Jordan, Elijah and Elisha were separated. He ascended by a whirlwind; very few people actually saw it. Elisha was the only one in the immediate vicinity. The sons of the prophets were probably at a distance, but did not understand the significance of what they were seeing. They could not share the experience —they were on the opposite bank of the Jordan. In Psalm 103:7 we read David's words:

> *He made known His WAYS to Moses,*
> *His ACTS to the sons of Israel.*

Witnessing a miracle isn't enough to constitute being in God's flow. The sons of Israel saw many signs and wonders, but their hearts were dull and their eyes dim. They grumbled and died in the wilderness. Moses, however, learned to walk in fellowship with God in the desert. In the solitary places Moses learned the ways of God. The sons of the prophets saw the acts but didn't understand their significance. Elisha was where God wanted him to be and was learning the ways of the Lord! Multitudes flock to see miracles today. They want to watch someone perform some feat of power in the Name of the Lord. But those who ultimately are used of God find themselves stripped of the excitement of miraculous things and are caught up in pleasing God. Somewhere beyond the Jordan experience, contemporary Elishas have been learning the ways of the Lord in the wilderness. They may APPEAR to be doing very little, but they have been allowing God to invest grace in their lives. They are learning to be adaptable and pliable in the hand of the Lord! The hour is coming upon us when these in obscurity will emerge with a brilliance. It is happening all over the continent and in many parts of the world. They are staying close to the moving of God and the leading of His Spirit even when it seems the "excitement" is wearing off. Just like Elisha.

Chapter Eight

Grief Before Growth!

*T*hen he took hold of his own clothes and tore
them in two pieces. He also took up the mantle
of Elijah that fell from him and returned and
stood by the bank of the Jordan. And he took the mantle of
Elijah that fell from him, and struck the waters and said,
"Where is the Lord, the God of Elijah?" And when he also
had struck, they were divided here and there; and Elisha
crossed over. (2 Kin. 2:12b-14)

The sons of the prophets watched from a distance as Elijah
was taken from Elisha. Elisha mourned the loss. Those at a
distance cannot appreciate loss until it touches them personally.
How empty these men were. Many in charismatic circles today
are equally empty. They are not touched by the hurts or the

needs of others. They know nothing of the compassion of Christ. Remember the story of the Greeks who wanted to see Jesus? They had heard about His miracles and His ministry and they came to the disciples and said, "We would see Jesus!" Do people want to see Jesus today? Isaiah said He had no stately form or majesty that we should be attracted to Him (Is. 53:2). Jesus had an interesting message for those who wanted to see Him.

> *...unless a grain of wheat falls into the earth and dies, it remains by itself alone; but if it dies, it bears much fruit. He who loves his life loses it; and he who hates his life in this world shall keep it to life eternal. If anyone serves Me, let him follow Me; and where I am, there shall My servant also be; if anyone serves Me, the Father will honor him.* (John 12:24-27)

Elisha suffered loss, but it was for the purpose of growth! If he hadn't torn his own clothes, he would never have been able to wear Elijah's mantle. New wine belongs in new wineskins! Elisha's ministry was changing. He had served faithfully as Elijah's minister and now was to fulfill the prophetic office himself. The very grief he experienced brought him into the fulfillment of his heart's desire. It is strange and wonderful how God works in our lives. We desperately want God to fulfill the desires of our hearts, but we seem to be totally mystified by the ways in which He actually answers our prayers. Once we obtain that for which we have made petition, He has done such a work in our lives that the answered prayer takes on new meaning. God uses the very prayers we pray to shape us into the design He intended for us.

Grief is common to all. At one time or another everyone experiences it. Eventually we stop grieving and move on. During the charismatic outpouring a number of churches experienced the blessing and presence of the Lord. Healings, miracles, spontaneous praise and gifts of the Spirit abounded. But many of those who experienced tremendous blessing began to experience tremendous shaking. Great upheaval took place. Why? Because churches fell asleep. God was moving in many areas, so it was assumed that He was pleased. This was an unsafe assumption. Convinced that God could only move in the way they believed, they boxed Him out. Rules and regulations and by-laws became their gods. The anointing was lost.

I have seen too many churches that once experienced the glory of the Lord and now are empty shells. Convinced of their own self-righteousness, they condemned the very moving of God in their midst. There is a need for us to ask the question the disciples asked Jesus on the night He disclosed that one of them would betray Him: "Surely not I, Lord?" (See Mark 14:19.) Is it possible that some of us hinder the hand of God in our midst? Betrayal is a strong word, but perhaps an appropriate one. While none of us would ever advocate a church split, have we, by our attitudes, actually driven people away because we were so comfortable in our traditions? Were others of us torn in a church upheaval? Perhaps these have never again been able to find a local church to call home or to feel the same presence of the Lord. The faces are different, the atmosphere is different, the worship is different. Let's learn a lesson from Elisha. Surely he grieved; however, there comes a time when we must stop grieving and begin to act.

You may be in a church right now that hasn't tasted half of what you once had. You may feel isolated and alone. Don't rebel against the leadership; don't grumble and complain. Don't look back any more. God has allowed you to taste something great and glorious. You haven't lost that! It's all there inside, waiting to explode! Go back and stand by the banks of the Jordan. Take up the mantle that has fallen. Stop waiting for God to move through someone else. Lay hold of that for which you were apprehended by Christ Jesus and begin to pour your heart out to God. Cast all your cares upon Him. But don't stop there! Take the mantle. It's lying at your feet. Have faith in God. He who parted the waters of the Jordan in times past will part them again. Like Elisha of old, STRIKE THE WATERS. Some of us are going to wait forever for the next move of God and we'll never see it! God is waiting for *us* to move! If we will dare in this hour to take the mantle of delegated Kingdom authority and in the Name of the Lord Jesus Christ strike the waters of apathy, resistance and unbelief, the waters of fear and satanic strongholds that hinder God's Spirit, we shall find that the God of Elijah will move in our behalf. He shall make a way where there is no way! He shall cause the waters to part and we shall cross over on dry ground! Hallelujah!

Chapter Nine

Love Releases...Fear Possesses!

*N*ow when the sons of the prophets who were
at Jericho opposite him saw him, they said,
"The spirit of Elijah rests on Elisha." And
they came to meet him and bowed themselves to the ground
before him. And they said to him, "Behold now, there are
with your servants fifty strong men, please let them go and
search for your master; perhaps the Spirit of the Lord has
taken him up and cast him on some mountain or into some
valley." And he said, "You shall not send." But when they
urged him until he was ashamed, he said, "Send." They sent
therefore fifty men; and they searched three days, but did
not find him. And they returned to him while he was staying
at Jericho; and he said to them, "Did I not say to you, 'Do
not go'?" (2 Kin. 2:15-18)

Have you ever desired to be used of God in ministry? Have you longed in your heart to be His hand extended? Have you ever considered the struggles of those in ministry? It isn't all glorious. Some of us would like to think so, but God will ultimately burst our bubbles for our own good. Elisha was a different man after he crossed the Jordan. He would never be the same. Elisha inherited the sons of the prophets — and they had *not* crossed the Jordan. They were spiritually void of any insight at all. They confirmed their incompetence in these verses. Here was Elisha, fulfilling the call of God, and his congregation wanted their old pastor! Why is it that some people seem to grow in the things of God and others never quite get there?

The Lord is doing a new thing and some "unknowns" are speaking on behalf of the Lord. They have a message, but quite a few people want to hear it from someone of more prominence. This can be frustrating and discouraging. What we have from God will be proven. God will reward! The sons of the prophets shamed Elisha into sending them to look for Elijah. Elisha knew he was gone, but he couldn't convince them. They had to find it out for themselves. This is the same today! Don't try to defend your position; God is your strength and a saving defense to His anointed! (Ps. 28:8) Don't become angry at those who won't receive you, either. Love them and let them go. We must respond correctly to rejection. An improper response can bring resentment, anger and bitterness. And bitterness will not only defile you, but others as well (Heb. 12:15).

The sons of the prophets searched for Elijah for three days. The number three is symbolic of completion and perfection. (Examples: Jesus was three days in the grave; Jonah was three nights in the belly of the whale.) The inner prompting in the sons of the prophets had to run its course. What was Elisha doing during this time? Was he grumbling, resentful or bitter? No. He was calmly awaiting their return in Jericho. The only way to overcome resentments, rejection and bitterness is to remain in Jericho. Jericho is the picture of ultimate victory through praise and worship! When negative feelings begin to sink into your mind and disturb your heart, go to Jericho for three days. David declared:

Bless the Lord, O my soul; And ALL that is within me... (Ps. 103:1)

That "all" includes the temptation to pity oneself, to feel rejected, and to become angry or bitter. Like Elisha, we need to come back to Jericho and remain until the work is done. Before we cross the Jordan it is easy to cling to those feelings, but after crossing we give place to those things no longer because they hinder God's Spirit in us.

Lately many ministries have endured unjust criticism. Division has sprung up as a result. The Church must not allow such things! One message of God to the Church is shown through Elisha's return to Jericho. Let the words of the apostle Peter ring true in our hearts:

For this finds favor, if for the sake of conscience toward God a man bears up under sorrows when suffering unjustly.

For what credit is there if, when you sin and are harshly treated, you endure it with patience? But if when you do what is right and suffer for it you patiently endure it, this finds favor with God. For you have been called for this purpose, since Christ also suffered for you, leaving you an example for you to follow in His steps, who committed no sin, nor was any deceit found in His mouth; and while being reviled, He did not revile in return; while suffering, He uttered no threats, but kept entrusting Himself to Him who judges righteously... (1 Pet. 2:19-23)

Chapter Ten

Purifying the Waters!

*T*hen the men of the city said to Elisha, "Behold
now, the situation of this city is pleasant, as
my lord sees; but the water is bad, and the
land is unfruitful" [lit., "causes barrenness"]. *And he said,
"Bring me a new jar, and put salt in it." So they brought it
to him. And he went out to the spring of water, and threw
salt in it and said, "Thus says the Lord, 'I have purified
these waters; there shall not be from there death or unfruit-
fulness any longer.' " So the waters have been purified to
this day, according to the word of Elisha which he spoke.*
(2 Kin. 2:19)

In assessment of the charismatic movement, I would say,
"The situation of the city is pleasant, but the water is bad and
the land is unfruitful." It seems like a contradiction, doesn't it?

How can something be both pleasant and unfruitful? Many good things have occurred in the charismatic movement; people have been saved, healed, filled with the Spirit, and many have been freed from the torments of the enemy. But God wants to take what He has given us and cause it to touch the world! The great revivals of the past have had a tremendous impact on the world. Visitation from God does not accomplish all He intends if we fail to impact society. Oh, we have spent a great deal of time trying to change things outwardly; but what man needs is a reconstruction of his inner nature! Lobbying to change laws will never change the heart of man. The Church described in the Book of Acts only got involved in politics when their moral ethics conflicted with those of the state.

In spite of our church growth and satellite ministries, sin abounds and iniquity prevails. Fighting to change the laws of the land may do some good, but a goat will always be a goat, even if you try to make him look like a sheep. What is God asking of the Church today? Why aren't we functioning with the same power as the Church of the Book of Acts? We hear a great deal of talk about those who boast of having "New Testament" churches. Where is this New Testament Church? I am sure that there are many ministries in the land today that are attempting to build according to the apostolic pattern. But for the Church to be functioning and restored to the power of the first century ministry there must be a purifying of our methods. We must return to the ancient pathways and the age-old foundations (Is. 58:12). We must build upon the foundation of Christ and His principles. The Church is the

COVENANT COMMUNITY. In the Old Testament, Zion was the picture of the glory of God resting with His people. Zion speaks of the New Testament Church. Hebrews 12:22 declares that we, the Church, have come unto Mount Zion! It is a picture of the Church in all her glory and power. Many are crying out to God for a return to the pattern of the Book of Acts. How do we get there? In Second Kings 2:20 Elisha asks for two things: a new jar and salt. With these two ingredients the water was purified and the land was restored. The word "new" is significant in Scripture. The psalmist exhorts us to

Sing unto the Lord a NEW song. (Ps. 96:1)

The word "new" here implies something fresh and alive. Paul reminds us that if any man be in Christ, he is a NEW creation (2 Cor. 5:17). I can't help sensing in my spirit that God is wanting to do a new thing in the earth. Remember Isaiah's prophecy as recorded in Isaiah 43:18-19a:

Do not call to mind the former things,
Or ponder things of the past.
Behold, I will do something NEW,
Now it will spring forth;
Will you not be aware of it?

If our eyes are on the former things that God has done, we will not be aware of the new things He is desiring to do. The early outpourings of the Spirit of this century had their place and purpose, but many of those who were part of that move of God have opposed anything that has followed.

In the 1950's the great healing revivalists came to the

forefront of the Pentecostal movement. Several men rose to places of prominence and formed crusade-oriented ministries that took them around the globe. When their day was over, many of them could not accept the loss of fame and began using gimmickry to sustain their ministries. These men and women had genuine callings from the Lord. But the intent of God has not been one-man-ministries. When God began to balance this aspect of the charismatic movement in the late sixties and early seventies, an awareness of Body ministry emerged.

In spite of a new awareness, the city may be pleasant to the outward eye, but the land is unfruitful. Much of the reason for this is the need for God to do something NEW. Elisha asked for a *new* jar. Didn't Jesus call the Jews unto something new? But how hard it was for the Pharisees and scribes to release their traditions! Yet Jesus made it perfectly clear:

> *Nor do men put NEW wine into old wineskins; otherwise the wineskins burst, and the wine pours out, and the wineskins are ruined; but they put new wine into fresh wineskins, and both are preserved.* (Matt. 9:17)

New wine needs new wineskins. Why did the outpouring of the 1960's and '70's not bring about a greater impact? Because men have sought to put new wine into old wineskins. What are old wineskins? Outmoded tradition and denominational, sectarian spirits that have prevailed in the Church for centuries. We have tried to contain the move of God within a denominational setting. As a result, the sectarian spirit has produced an elitism among established denominations as well as newer "independent" fellowships that are more denominational than they care to admit. Some claim to have the true concept of local church autonomy, while others claim to have revelation of the fulness of the Spirit, as still others claim that they are the only ones who "worship the Father in spirit and truth"! There is even a sect of Christendom that claims to have the revelation on church government, and that all who do not embrace that revelation are going to hell. All these "revelations" have produced a snobby, stuffy, self-centered, fleshly PARTY SPIRIT consciousness that denies the heart of the Lord the joy of seeing us made one even as He and the Father are one (John 17).

God loves us all! He loves His children whether they are in a denominational church or a nondenominational church (between which I am not convinced there is much difference in the majority of cases). What God does not love, and in fact hates, is DENOMINATIONALISM. This is the revived Babylonian spirit seeking to destroy the work of Christ. Denominationalism has kept the Body of Christ divided for centuries. We have failed the Lord. If Jesus is coming soon, He must do a quick work because the Bride is not ready! Why have we designated the job of bringing the Church into unity to God when He had given it to us? If we are waiting for God to do something that we have been called to do, then it will never get done. The prophet Amos said that two cannot walk together except they be agreed (3:3). The crux of that revelation is this: God says, "I am the Lord, I change not!" If we expect to walk in agreement with God, we must realize that God isn't going to change. Who has to change? We do; we have no choice.

The denominational spirit is nothing new. It existed in the early days of the Church. In Acts 1:8 Jesus gave a mandate to

His disciples as He was ascending to the throne to await the time when every enemy is made a footstool for His feet. He said very clearly:

> *...but you shall receive power when the Holy Spirit has come upon you; and you shall be My witnesses both in Jerusalem, and in all Judea and Samaria, and even to the remotest part of the earth.* (Acts 1:8)

Note the progression: Jerusalem, Judea, Samaria and the farthest point on the globe. When God birthed the Church in power, it was glorious. The Spirit of God came and fulfilled the Feast of Pentecost, and thousands were ingathered as a result. The Jerusalem Church grew to over 8,000 within the first few months. Tremendous miracles, signs and wonders accompanied the apostolic ministry. Unfortunately, the Jerusalem Church grew comfortable and fat. The fault lay with the leadership.

In Acts chapter ten Peter received a vision while he was asleep on a rooftop in Joppa. This vision demanded Peter's REPENTANCE. God wanted to bring the gospel to the Gentiles, but Peter was too proud to oblige, since as a Jew he was "pure" and the Gentiles were unclean. Jesus had already disclosed that the gospel eliminated the "chosen race" concept. Calvary was for everybody! Peter and James, however, were proud Jews. Proud of their heritage, proud of their lineage, proud of the fact that they had been entrusted with the oracles of God. Peter had seen Jesus minister to the Roman centurion (Matt. 8:5-13) and had heard Jesus marvel at the faith of this Gentile. He heard Jesus say,

...many shall come from east and west, and recline at the table with Abraham, Isaac, and Jacob, in the kingdom of heaven. (Matt. 8:11)

Peter heard, but did not perceive. In John chapter four we see Jesus reaching out to the Samaritan woman. The Jews *never* dealt with Samaritans! Peter saw the revival brought to Samaria through that one woman. But his heart was still hard. After three incidents he still didn't understand and received a rebuke from the Lord. He did go to the house of Cornelius in obedience, but with great reservation. When we read the first few chapters of the Book of Acts, we tend to read as if it were a motion picture moving rapidly along. If that were true, we could forgive Peter his reluctance to obey the Lord. The tragedy is this: Peter received this vision at least eight or nine *years* after the ascension of the Lord!

After nine years the church leadership had done nothing to extend the message to fulfill the mandate of Acts 1:8. They were content to stay in the confines of their own little revelation.

Why do you suppose Stephen had to be the first martyr of the Church? The answer is in Acts 11:19:

So then those who were SCATTERED because of the persecution that arose in connection with Stephen made their way to Phoenicia and Cyprus and Antioch...

Do you see the sovereign hand of God? The church at Jerusalem had grown inward, sectarian and denominational. They refused to move in times of peace, so God sent a time of persecution. The very enemies of the gospel were the instrument God used to scatter the seed. Stephen's death led to widespread persecution, which in turn led to a scattering of the believers. God was tired of playing church; there was work to be done. Jesus had told the believers to go to Jerusalem, Judea, Samaria and the whole planet. The Church had not even gotten beyond *Judea* during the first eight or nine years! Within a matter of days after the stoning of Stephen and the scattering of the Church, Philip brought revival to Samaria, and the rest went to conquer the world (Phoenicia, Cyprus, Antioch, etc.).

How crucial it is that we understand this! King Cyrus of Persia was an enemy of God's people, but in Isaiah he is called "Cyrus Mine anointed"! Why? Because God will use whatever is necessary to bring His people out of the old and into the new. Some of the churches that were the largest centers for the charismatic revival have been whittled down to nothing in the past few years. Is it possible that somewhere we have failed to fully obey the purpose for which God raised up a mighty work?

Many churches today are struggling and failing to fulfill God's purposes. Until the leadership takes responsibility for the problems and begins to exercise delegated authority in a responsible and godly manner, these churches will struggle endlessly, until the people are burned out and have lost all vision. Proverbs 29:18 tells us that without a progressive vision the people perish.

We reproduce after our kind in the spiritual as well as the natural. In Acts 11:19 (after the dispersion), Luke tells us that some of the disciples that fled to Phoenicia, Cyprus and Antioch were

...speaking the word to NO ONE EXCEPT TO JEWS ALONE.

Somehow these disciples of the apostles at Jerusalem got the impression that the gospel was only for the Jews. Peter and James had reproduced the sectarian spirit in their disciples! Who were Paul's biggest troublemakers? The Judaizers. They were part of the original sect of the church at Jerusalem, preaching circumcision and observance of the Mosaic law as essential to salvation in Christ. Every place Paul went with the message, the Judaizers followed close behind to leaven the lump with their heresy. And it's still heresy!

Paul told the church at Galatia that Peter's sectarian spirit, as well as that of James' disciples, was hypocrisy and a stumbling block. Paul maintained that any gospel other than his gospel was false, and that those who preach any such were accursed. We are not saying that Peter was preaching a false gospel, but his failure to make a clean break with Judaism led to a legalistic spirit that became worse in the following generation of believers. What was allowed by the Jerusalem apostles in slight moderation produced an excess in their disciples. On the positive side, however, Luke reveals in Acts 11:20:

But there were some of them, men of Cyprus and Cyrene, who came to Antioch and began speaking to the Greeks also, preaching the Lord Jesus.

God still had a group that was obedient to the original intent of the message, and as a result the church at Antioch was birthed. The Antioch church became the very platform from which the program of God was to be launched to evangelize the world.

To reiterate, God wants to do a new thing in the earth. That new thing is no different today than it was 2,000 years ago!

We simply fall into the trap of the old fleshly pseudo religious ways of doing things. We get far too comfortable with our programs, our plans, our accomplishments; and when new direction emerges, we are reticent to change. I am sure God grows weary with the "sons of the prophets" because we need to be broken out of the mold.

The church at Antioch serves as a model for what God wants to accomplish in every local church. Let's look at Acts chapters eleven and thirteen to see if perhaps the idea behind "new wineskins" is explained.

When the scattered believers preached to the Greeks in Antioch, they preached this message: the LORD JESUS. The foundation of faith in the New Covenant is the Lordship of Christ. Christ was exalted following His death and resurrection to be LORD! How desperately the Church needs to reevaluate her foundation. Only one foundation will endure the shaking that is upon us and will increase in the days ahead. That foundation is the LORDSHIP OF CHRIST. When Jesus turned the water into wine at the wedding in Cana, Mary told the servants:

Whatever He says to you, do it. (John 2:5)

The Church needs to come to this place of being obedient to Christ in all He requires. This obedience must be in leadership as well as laity. Churches have too long been built around the personality of man rather than the Christ of glory. In Revelation 21:23 we find that the only light in the City of God is the light of the Lamb. There is no natural light in the Holiest of All, only the light of God's glory. No flesh shall glory in His presence. God is stripping and shaking us so that only the light of His glory remains!

An exciting observation about the church at Antioch is that it was founded by ordinary believers, not big personalities. In addition to an understanding of the lordship of Christ, they took personal responsibility for evangelizing the lost. God wants to bring a great harvest before the coming of the Lord, but believers must evangelize! God hasn't called the big names to win the lost; in fact, if we read Ephesians 4:11-13 in context, we find that the purpose of the evangelist is to teach the sheep to evangelize! Sheep reproduce sheep! Thank God for the fresh emphasis in our day to equip believers to evangelize.

After the church in Antioch was formed, the Jerusalem church heard and commissioned Barnabas to oversee it, setting things in order. Barnabas was not an opportunist! The Body of Christ has seen many who seek their own gain rather than the riches of Christ. Thank God that Barnabas was sent and not one who might have possessed a legalistic spirit (an unfortunate characteristic of the church in Jerusalem). The name *Barnabas* means "encourager."

Barnabas had an apostolic mantle. Ephesians 4:11 discloses God's five-fold ministry. Few function in this order as God intends. As an apostolic minister, Barnabas came to help set the house of God at Antioch in order. Notice how he accomplishes this:

Then when he had come and witnessed the grace of God, he rejoiced and began to encourage them all with resolute heart to remain true to the Lord... (Acts 11:23)

Three keys reveal why Barnabas was so well received. Scripture says he:

1. witnessed the grace of God — In other words, he came

and saw that God was alive and well in the church and had
been doing fine before he arrived. He came and OBSERVED
that truth. He readily recognized that there was tangible grace
manifested in the believers there.

2. rejoiced — Barnabas shared in their joy and joined in
the excitement of it. (I trust a pattern is beginning to emerge in
your thinking.)

3. began to encourage them all — His vocal ministry was
one of encouragement. He didn't quench their zeal. He didn't
say, "Stop evangelizing until we mature the baby sheep we
have already." The only demand he placed on them was obedience to God ("...remain true to the Lord").

Luke goes on to say that the reason Barnabas had such an
effective ministry was that...

he was a good man, and full of the Holy Spirit and of faith.
And considerable numbers were brought to the Lord. (Acts
11:24)

There is no doubt that a mighty move of God was occurring,
and when Barnabas arrived he encouraged an explosion!
But notice verse 25:

And he left for Tarsus to look for Saul...

Why would someone involved in a growing, healthy work
leave right in the midst of it? Barnabas realized he could not
handle the leadership alone! It takes a humble man to realize
he doesn't have every gift of the Spirit to shepherd the flock of
God. Barnabas realized that one man can't fill every gap to
oversee God's house.

Many fine men have been burned out because they tried to do the job all alone. This has a disastrous effect. The Body is never fully nourished by that which every joint supplies and therefore becomes imbalanced. The minister never comes to maturity by being sharpened by his co-ministers. When the sheep come to this realization, they despise his authority and he loses the sheep as well! How desperately the Body needs a balance in leadership through team ministry. Team members play for the benefit of the whole. But if one member hogs the ball, the rest of the team loses heart. In a multiple staff situation where team members are stifled by the insecurity of the senior man, the seeds of rebellion are sown and the Body is fragmented. Barnabas points out that we *need each other.*

When Barnabas found Saul he brought him back to Antioch, and they taught as a team for an entire year. In order for Barnabas to feel free enough to leave Antioch in search of Saul, he had to be confident in the leadership that already existed. It is obvious that Barnabas had raised up eldership in the time he was there. We have no idea how long Barnabas was away from Antioch, but it was obviously for a season. Luke implies that Barnabas didn't know where Saul would be and it took a while to find him.

Barnabas hadn't seen Saul for twelve to fourteen years at this point. Think for a moment about Saul. He is a persecutor of the Church, is in hearty agreement with the stoning of Stephen, has a dramatic conversion on the Damascus road and is given a mighty call to preach the gospel before kings and princes. After such a great revelation, he finds himself for fourteen years in the wilderness in Tarsus, making tents. In Second Corinthians 11:24-27, Paul recounts many of his sufferings to the Corinthian church, including receiving the thirty-nine lashes fives times from the Jews. A careful study of the life of the apostle reveals that much of his persecution took place at the hands of Jews in the wilderness of Tarsus. He returned to his own hometown proclaiming Jesus, and the rabbis called him a blasphemer and ordered him scourged (almost to death). Tradition states that his wife deserted him as a result of his new-found faith.

So Saul found nothing in Judaism to hang on to. He saw clearly the fruit of legalism. For fourteen years in the wilderness God was not only rooting out the legalistic spirit that blinded the Jews, He was driving home the full intent of the gospel and the revelation of the glorious Church and the New Jerusalem. The pattern for the true Zion of God was being birthed in the Tarsus wilderness for fourteen years, awaiting the timing of God for the revelation to be fully received. God had to shift centers from Jerusalem to Antioch and prepare a new people untouched by tradition (the Gentiles) to mold the new things He was doing. When the time was ripe, God stirred Barnabas to search for Saul and bring him to the forefront of the new move of God. Antioch was ready for Saul and Saul was ready for Antioch. This could not have happened fourteen years previously in Jerusalem; the people of God weren't ready.

God has been preparing a people in this day. They haven't been molded in the traditions of former visitations. They are hungry for truth. God has also been grooming ministries in the wilderness of Tarsus. Every ounce of legalism is being driven out of them and the full understanding of the Person and the work of Christ is being imparted, to result in the production of a revelation of God's glory which is yet to be seen!

At Antioch Saul and Barnabas taught for an entire year and revival continued. The disciples were first called "Christians" at Antioch. There was something so radically new about this visitation that believers inherited a new name. "Jew" belonged to the older. God has now brought Jew and Gentile together! In Isaiah 62:2 the prophet, speaking of God's chosen people, says this:

...And you will be called by a new name,
Which the mouth of the Lord will designate.

At Antioch the disciples, the chosen generation of First Peter 2:9, are called by a new name — "CHRISTIANS." A *Christian* is one who is "like Christ." There was something recognized in the company of believers that caused the citizens of Antioch to say they were like Christ. The Church, the house of God, bore the resemblance of the character of the Builder.

Christ has given apostles and prophets (Eph. 4:11). God still has prophets who declare a holy and righteous standard and move in a revelational realm with a word of knowledge to reveal past, present and future events. God will not do anything without first revealing it to His prophets (Amos 3:7). Please recognize that God prepared His Church while the world was in darkness! The key to this is obedience. The Church recognized the prophetic anointing and obeyed the word that came forth.

Fear pervades people's hearts regarding prophetic ministry, perhaps because of abuse that has been labeled "prophetic." However, there is always a danger of throwing out the good with the bad. That danger must have existed in the early

Church, because Paul, in writing to the church at Thessolonica, says this:

Do not DESPISE prophetic utterances. But examine every-thing carefully; HOLD FAST to that which is good. (1 Thess. 5:20-21)

Here is the balance. There are many men in ministry who embrace the truths of the five-fold ministry and the gifts of the Spirit, but will not allow them to function. The reason behind this, they say, can be supported Scripturally; but I suspect a negative predisposition to the gifts. We need to allow prophetic ministry to bring the word of God to the Body, and we need to obey the word when it comes! For if we do not obey, we will pay the price. What if a prophet arises like Jim Jones; do we all commit suicide when he says so? There have always been and will be those who lead others astray. But in God's house, if mature ministries are functioning together in the pattern of Ephesians 4:11 and keeping each other balanced in covenant relationship, we should see a healthy functioning of the prophetic ministry in the midst of God's people.

These are decision-making days. No need for deep theolo-gical debates; it is a simple issue of faith in the integrity of the word of God. God says He gave us apostles and prophets. Where are they? They are functioning where they are recog-nized and received as such and allowed to minister.

Acts chapter thirteen points out that there is no room in the New Covenant Church for a one-man show. God's order for the Church is plurality with ONE CHIEF AMONG EQUALS. I have an anointing in one area of ministry, you have an anoint-ing in another. How foolish and presumptuous of me to tell you how to function in your anointing. In Antioch prophets and teachers functioned together as a team: Barnabas, originally from Jerusalem; Simeon, who most likely was the black man who carried the cross of Christ up the Via Dolorosa (Luke 23:26); Lucius, also of Cyrene; Manaen, a wealthy in-law of King Herod; and Saul of Tarsus.

Antioch was a metropolitan city; a melting pot, if you will. The eldership represented every strata of society. In God's house all were equal. While a Roman soldier singles out a black man to carry an ignominious cross upon which the Savior would be crucified (racial prejudice ran rampant even then), in the house of God Simeon is exalted to a place of rulership over the Father's affairs. Hallelujah! Manaen, though quite wealthy according to historians, shares equality with others and ministers in the house of the Lord. Each elder had a unique ministry. Their various backgrounds, nationalities and occupations shaped the effectiveness of the ministry of the church in Antioch.

We are told in Acts 13:2 that they ministered to the Lord. They were worshipers! There is truth in worship that must be experienced. God is seeking worshipers in this hour! We need to learn how to minister unto the Lord. "Minister" here was a word used by the Greeks to describe service to the city or state above and beyond normal obligations. A Greek citizen, in addition to having a job and paying taxes, was required to donate his services above and beyond the call of duty to the body politic. This service was called the act of MINISTRY. In our day it could mean jury duty or volunteer help in a social or civic organization. In the house of God, besides our responsibilities to the King, that which goes above and beyond is WORSHIP. The writer to the Hebrews puts it this way:

Through HIM then [all acceptable worship is through Christ by the power of the Spirit], *let us CONTINUALLY offer up a sacrifice of praise to God, that is, the fruit of lips that give thanks to His name.* (Heb. 13:15)

God is looking for a Church committed to worship. Some have made a ritual of worship and worship worship! God wants us to worship HIM! We are living in a day when God wants to purify us. Worship releases the new wine.

The eldership and the body at Antioch also fasted and prayed. How we need to have seasons of fasting and prayer in the Church! During fasting and prayer direction came to the church at Antioch. We are told in Acts 13:2:

While they were...fasting, the Holy Spirit said...

How did the Holy Spirit say what He said? Through the *prophets!* Prophetic ministry yielded to God, pointed the direction, and said, "This is the way, walk ye in it."

An atmosphere of worship and prayer will bring the prophetic anointing to a people committed to covenant relationship in the house of God.

The word of the Lord that came to Antioch through Saul and Barnabas was to be sown elsewhere as well. God has been stirring up His Body to plant new works all over the land in our day. Apostolic understanding is arising in local churches that realize that even as sheep reproduce sheep, so churches can reproduce churches. The church at Antioch reproduced itself. Unlike the Jerusalem apostles, these men went all over the world with their message.

If traditional churches will not embrace what God is doing, God will release the five-fold ministry in new works. The church at Antioch was not afraid to lose two key men because the leadership had done such a good job of raising up ministry that the church flourished regardless.

Saul and Barnabas were sent out by the laying on of hands; commissioned not merely by the Spirit, but with the witness and blessing of the local church as well. Many traveling ministries would do well to evaluate their purpose for going out. Many of these ministries would bear more fruit if they were plugged into a local church and functioning in a team effort. Notice also that no ministry was sent out alone. Saul and Barnabas were a team. It is my conviction that the face of itinerant ministry will change radically in the days ahead as the Church comes to grips with the true purpose of traveling ministry. If such ministry is to survive in the coming days, those involved will have to reprioritize and reevaluate their purposes and see if they are fulfilling Ephesians 4:11-12. The Church needs to realize that most souls that need to be saved aren't going to be in the meetings; they're going to be out on the streets. It seems to me that plane fare, housing, and an honorarium for one soul to be saved in a service is poor stewardship of God's money. But if the money spent to bring in the speaker is invested in teaching the sheep how to reproduce, then it's money well spent!

The Body of Christ is in a time of transition. It is time for new wineskins. We need a new vessel to contain the new vintage! Elisha asked for salt to be placed in the new jar. The New Testament Church is a community in covenant. We are related one to another through covenant. Numbers 18:19 speaks of a "covenant of salt." A covenant of salt was irrevocable and binding. We must be bound together by strong cords in this hour. We are too quick to run away from problems, from relationships, from confrontations. The Body needs to come together by a covenant of salt. In Leviticus 2:13, we see that salt was required by God in the offerings of the Temple. In ancient times its value was equal to gold.

Among Orientals salt has been used to ratify agreements. As such, salt is a symbol of fidelity, commitment and constancy. To God's people a covenant of salt was a reminder of the faithfulness required in the keeping of covenant. Jesus said:

> *Salt is good; but if the salt becomes unsalty, with what will you make it salty again? Have salt in yourselves and be at peace with one another.* (Mark 9:50)

Jesus reminded His disciples that they were — and WE ARE — the "salt of the earth" (Matt. 5:13). It was the salt that Elisha put in the new jar which caused the waters to be purified. Salt speaks of the Church, the covenant community in action. It speaks of loyalty and fidelity to Christ and to one another.

We have seen half-hearted commitment to unity in the local church. When things don't go our way, we pack our belongings and drag our frustrations to another church. The result is that we never grow up. The situations are new, but we are still the same. The root of our problems (if they have not been dealt with) will cause us to face them again and again until we settle down and let God purge them. We need to realize we have problems and need to change. We've been thinking the other guy has the problems and we pray for God to change him! The truth is that God wants to change *us*. This is easier said than done. Unity comes at a high price. What's the price? The right to have things my way all the time!

It can get pretty hot in the fire. God says the fire and heat are going to be turned up so that the gold can be purified! Heat brings impurities to the surface so they can be eliminated. According to Isaiah 4:4, God purges Zion by a spirit of judgment and a spirit of burning! If it gets hot where you are, there may be a reason. If you are loyal to God you'll endure the heat. If you are loyal to the Body and understand covenant commitment, you won't search out another church because you'll realize that God is turning up the fire there as well! In the presence of intense heat, salt will not dissolve. It can withstand extremes in temperature. The basis for unity is salt: loyalty and fidelity. Paul asked and admonished the church at Ephesus to be diligent to preserve the unity of the Spirit in the bond of peace. The word "preserve" means "to watch over" or "keep guard"; and "diligent" means an "aggressive earnestness and zeal." "Have salt," said Jesus, "and be at peace with one another." God wants to so work in us an attitude of loyalty and fidelity that the unity of the Spirit causes peace to prevail over the Church.

Why is unity so important? Remember that the water had to be purified first, and then the land reaped the blessing according to the word of Elisha. So it is in the Kingdom of God. Listen to Jesus as He prays for the Church:

> ...that they may all be ONE; even as Thou, Father, art in Me, and I in Thee, that they also may be in Us; that the WORLD MAY BELIEVE that Thou didst send Me. (John 17:21)

Salt leads to purification; loyalty and fidelity lead to unity. Unity leads to a release of the Spirit of God to those outside the

Kingdom. Through our expression of oneness, the glory of the risen Christ is revealed and many will believe.

May the Father of Glory move by His Spirit to empower us as His people to embrace the principles of Elisha. Let's move on to see His glory revealed in the land!